Granny's Golden Nuggets

Volume One

Granny's Golden Nuggets

Volume One

By: Erma Cooper

Dedication

I want to dedicate this book to my grandchildren whom I love so much and who are my inspiration. I also want to dedicate this book to all the grandchildren in the world. Those who live their life according to the wisdom that was passed down divinely by their grandma, granny, nana, or other endearing nicknames you call your grandmother.

Acknowledgements

I thank God, our Heavenly Father, who blessed me with three loving and talented sisters: Angela with technology and proof-reading skills; Alise with visionary artistic creativity; and Lillian with proof-reading and editing skills. It was an honor to have their input and help with completing this book project.

Table of Contents

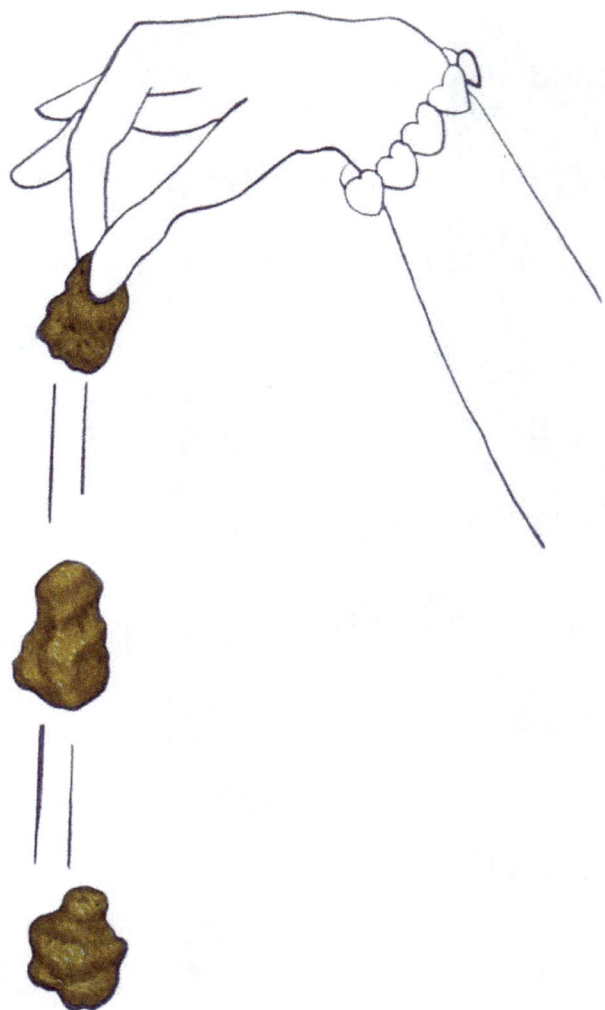

Golden Nuggets 1:

"Power Words"

Watch what you say, even when you are joking because you create what You Say.

Don't talk defeat even if it looks like it.

Speak positive words.

If you want to go to Heaven when you leave this earth, Always Think before you act or say anything.

Watch what you do and say – You never know who you are inspiring.

Squash any negative talk or actions; don't listen to it or react to it.

Your tongue sets in motion what happens to you. **Speak positive words to yourself.**

Let's just confess that we are having a **Wonderful Day**, no matter how it starts or looks.

Control how you respond to life's situations that are sent to destroy your **Peace**. Take a deep breath first and think about what **Jesus would say or do**.

Watch the words that come out of your mouth, don't let them **be idle or ignorant words**.

Life and **death** will happen so watch what you speak out of your mouth about yourself.

Well, I have learned that **Blessings** and **Cursing** shouldn't come out the same mouth, again **Watch What You Say**.

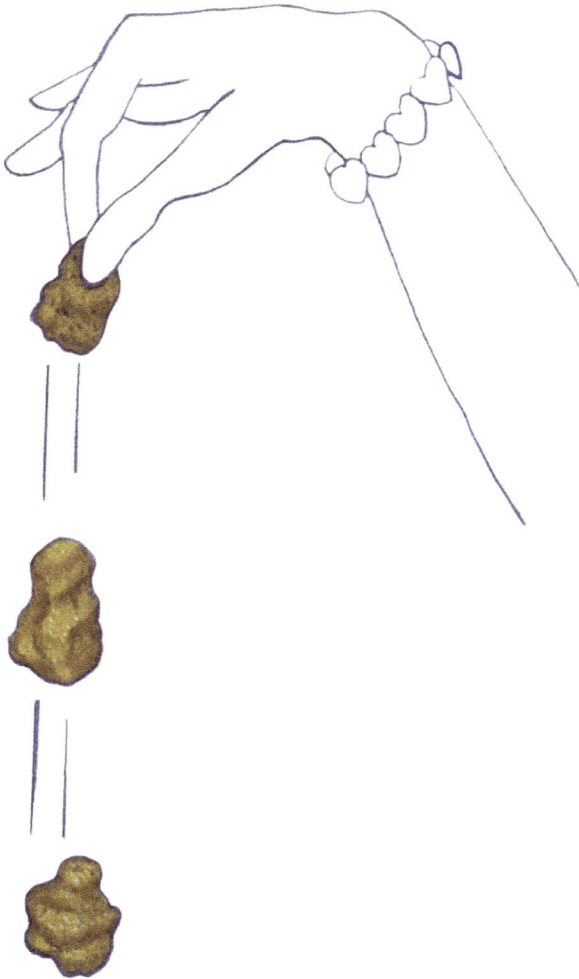

Golden Nuggets 2:

"Healthy Relationships"

Do unto everyone, whatever you want done to yourself.

Love others as you do yourself.

Do something nice for someone today, doesn't matter what it is.

Pick one person today to do something nice for that they would like. You reap what you sow.

Love and be kind to one another.

Remember when you show love it will come back with more LOVE.

Be kind to everyone, you never know what Battles they are fighting.

There will be times when the internet will go down but spending more time with your family is the greater Blessing.

We must Honor, Respect, and mostly Love one another.

Getting along with each other and family is essential to maintain a healthy family relationship.

A loving family is a force that can accomplish great things.

We are living in times when reaping what you sow is coming faster than ever. Be Mindful of how you treat people as well as what you do.

Today is an Awesome Day to be grateful and help someone who might be having a problem worse than yours. Be Blessed and Safe.

Love your birth family, as well as the family you choose.

When the season to Celebrate the Birth of Jesus arrives; please don't just be a gift receiver but be a gift giver of encouragement to someone who needs it.

Let's show more Love towards each other; whether they are your friend or relative or someone you don't know that well. Love! Love! Love!

There will be rainy days in your life. Just as God uses the rain to revitalize the earth. Our lives are revitalized when we show LOVE to others.

I can't express enough how important it is to love everyone no matter how challenging.

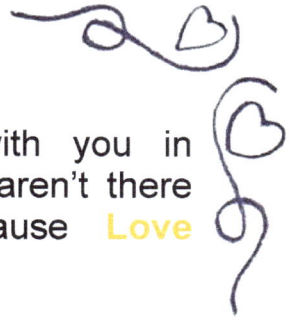

A **true friend** will be with you in difficult times even if they aren't there with you physically. Because **Love and Prayer Count.**

Tell the people in your life that you **appreciate them**, and never take them for granted; it could be the last time you see or hear from them.

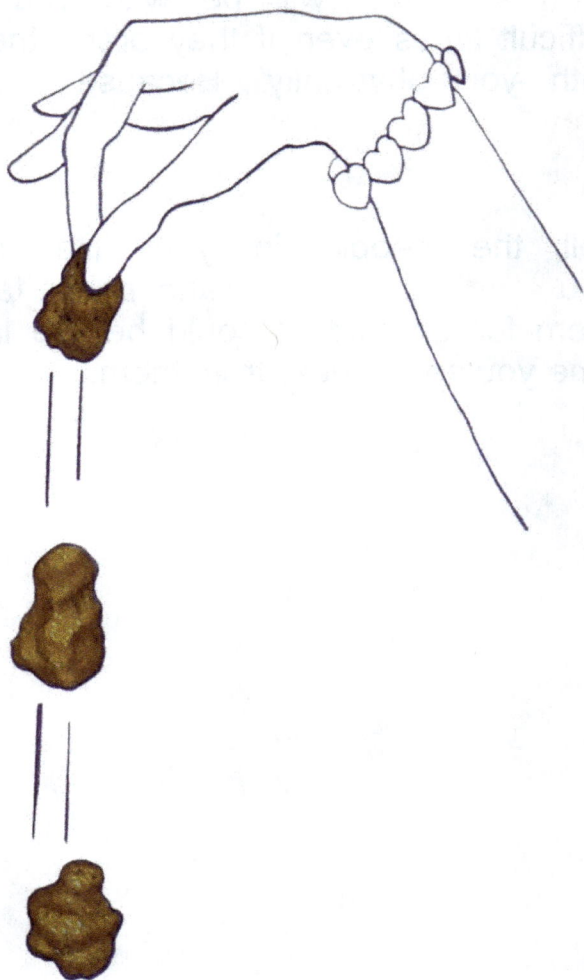

Golden Nuggets 3:

"Honor Thy Mother and Father"

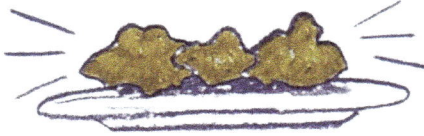

The Bible says Honor your Parents so that your days may be long upon the earth.

NEVER EVER YELL at your parents, curse them, or refer to them by any demeaning or derogatory name. It is important for Your Success as a decent person and getting into Heaven.

Today let's do something special for your PARENTS to let them know that they are loved and appreciated.

Parents are not Perfect, but they do love and protect you.

Remember your parent's Wedding Anniversary, be extra nice and do something special for them.

Life does not come with a manual; it comes with parents who are not perfect.

Parents are not always right, but they are human. They will sometimes make mistakes and they still deserve your love and respect.

Show your parents that you really care about them. Be an investigative reporter, interview them, ask them what's important to them and take notes. Then when you know what is important to them, act on it.

God loves us all no matter what! He is our example on How we should love and honor our parents.

Our parents are our tour guides to help us grow up. There are valuable life lessons along the way so pay attention during the tour.

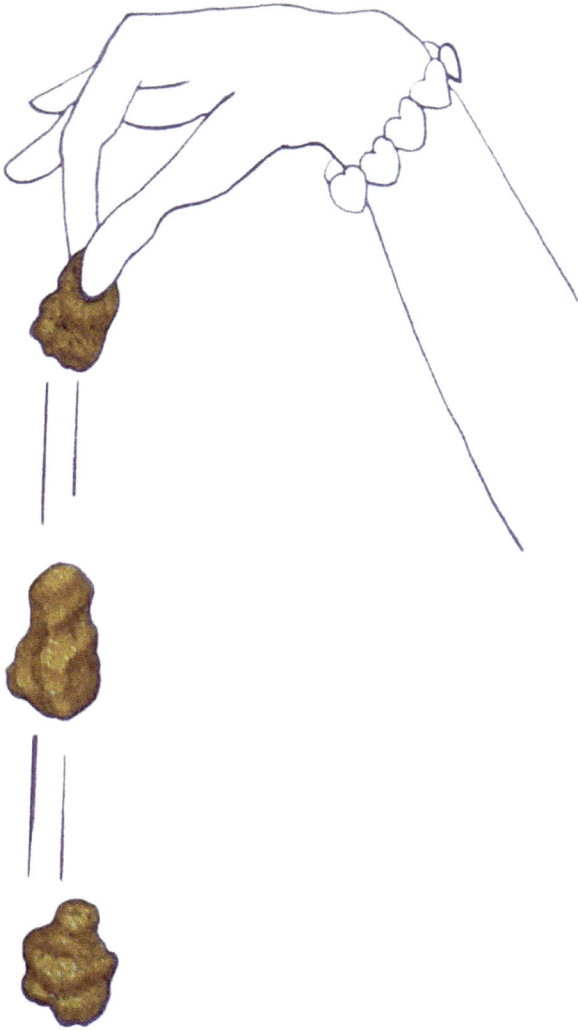

Golden Nuggets 4:

"Being a Better Me"

You are only **Responsible** for your own actions whether **Good or Bad**.

Don't let anything get you upset today, choose to shake it off and be **Happy**.

Stop looking at all the **Bad Things** that have happened to you. But instead look at all the **Good Things** that happen to you.

Work on being a better you; **smile, talk nicely, be friendly, and don't be negative**.

Life doesn't happen to you; Life happens for you **to grow** and **be better**.

#1 Be nice to yourself today. #2 Do a little something special for yourself. Remember you don't have to spend money to do #1 or #2.

Thoughts come to you all the time, but it is what you do with them that counts.

You must have a will to do what's right, focus on what's right, and be committed to what is right.

There will be things in life that will happen to you. You choose how you will allow what happened to affect your life. I suggest you take the bad things and turn them into a positive thing and THRIVE.

Life doesn't just happen to you, but what occurs helps to make you better.

Be mature. Be still first and think things out first before you act.

21

Always try to have a positive attitude even when it is difficult to maintain.

Think on something Pleasant while you are waiting on the unpleasant situation to change.

Don't always be quick to say how you feel about things you don't like or disagree with; learn to be quiet and weigh out the situation first.

Life is full of things we don't like or agree with; don't be a complainer. Allow life to give you another opportunity to create a better you.

Stop looking at where you are, it will hinder where you are going in life.

We can't always be winners in things we do; but we can always be winners in how we react to things we do and speak.

You have to pay attention to your **weaknesses**, so you don't keep making the same **mistakes**.

Never be **too proud** to say you are wrong. It builds **great character**.

Don't try **to impress people**. Be a **positive light** that impresses them.

Make sure you get your **rest**, don't get too busy to rest, it helps maintain your **good health**.

Whenever you get hurt, you have to get over it quickly. **Don't let it take over you - Love!!!**

Don't take everything **personally**; it is just the way some people are.

Rudeness is a weak person's strength; a strong person is **Polite** and shows **Love**.

Stop allowing small things to upset you; Practice self-control, Slow down and Think before you react.

Hurt people hurt other people. Knowing this can help you treat others with compassion if they are hurtful towards you.

Loving yourself as you do others is a Golden Rule, no matter who they are.

You need to walk away from all drama and the people who create it.

Surround yourself with people who make you laugh and happy.

Be true to yourself and believe that God loves you.

So many people from your past know a version of you that doesn't exist anymore. Don't let them take you backwards.

All the challenges of life come to teach us about ourselves and make us better people if we sit back and open our eyes and truly see.

Don't compare yourself to anyone else, just be better than the person you were yesterday.

Be a Joyful, Loving and Thoughtful person daily.

Saying "Thank You", can make someone's day. Try it! It's Nice to be Nice.

Examine yourself daily, to make sure nothing negative, evil, or destructive is coming from you...Only Love.

Everyone on earth has Problems from time to time, don't let them define you!!!

Each day we wake up is a fresh start, so we can move forward and heal from whatever went wrong yesterday.

The purpose of storms in your life is to purify you and knock off some of the rough edges.

Don't be judgmental, give a person a chance to show who they are.

Remember that we all make mistakes; we are a work in progress.

Love, Love, Love, we all need it and must show it throughout our day.

When giving up seems easy, HOLD ON! All things you receive take work and sacrifice.

Look and expect something good to happen to you every day and do something good every day.

Someone once told me that Life is hard and then you die. But even if it is, you can still have peace, joy, happiness, and love. You choose!!!!

Enjoy Life, don't sweat the small stuff, find a bright side, there is Always one if you look for it.

When you get frustrated with older people because of what they can't do, remember, if you live long enough, you will be an older person one day.

Let your character and how you live speak louder than what you say.

Take care of your body, watch what you eat, watch what you say about yourself, exercise, and get plenty of sleep. You only get one body; it affects you as you get older.

We all make mistakes, but they don't have to define who you are now, and, in the future. Mistakes can be forgiven.

This is the season to give and show love, we should do both.

Be a person that shows a positive gesture to everyone that you come in contact with throughout every season.

I had a conversation with a person about Forgiveness, this is what I learned. You might be surprised by how we can hold bitterness in us, just mention the name of a person who wronged you.

Forgiveness has to come from a conscious decision to want to be better and forgiven.

Don't beat yourself up about decisions you make in love, they will work out. God always knows your heart.

Having Patience is something we must have and practice no matter what.

You can't have un-forgiveness in your heart no matter what was done to you; it lets negative things happen to you.

There will be people that will upset you but be the better person. The rewards will be great.

I was born to be a Blessing, wherever I am.

Be happy to see someone get a Blessing; you could be next.

It is so interesting to see how the rain helps things grow, that's what situations of life do for us.

Don't take a substitute for the real thing, don't depend on your emotions in times of trouble.

Allow love, peace, forgiveness, and patience to be active in your life at all times because the attributes of God are everlasting.

It's so easy to become dependent on our cellphones for communication, knowledge, and entertainment that we forget to first check with God. Sometimes cellphones die but **GOD NEVER** dies.

Technology is the way of our world now. Please be careful how you use it because it could follow you for life.

Learn how to ALWAYS BE POSITIVE, when using any form of technology.

Do not let depression or sadness take over your mind, especially during the Holiday Season. Remember even if you have to look hard, there is something positive in your life.

Never let Pride get in the way of your life or people. We have to learn that we will never be perfect because perfection only comes from God.

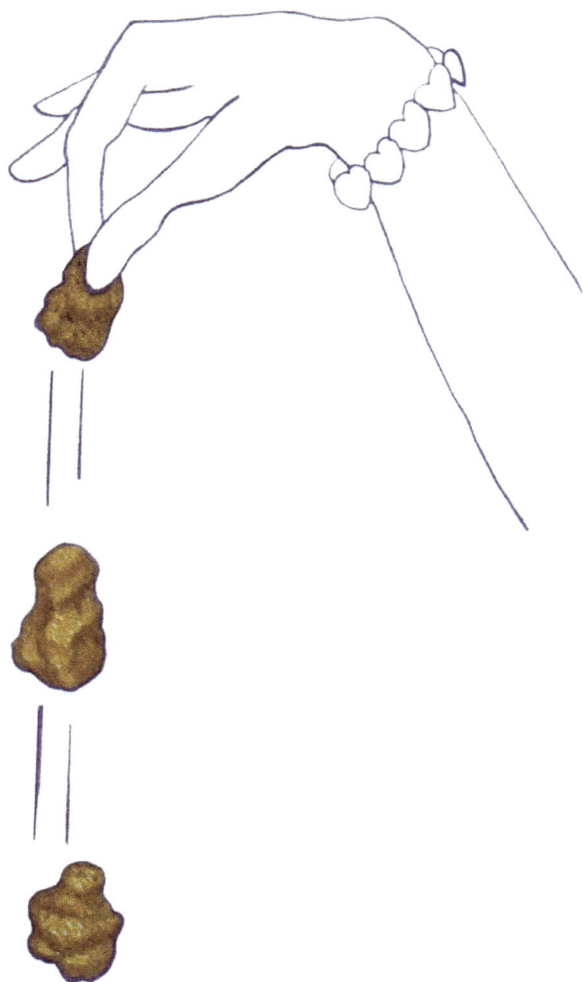

Golden Nuggets 5:

"Thankful Heart"

Tell the Lord "Thank You" for everything he does for you throughout the day.

Be thankful for your parents and honor them.

Today is Thankful Friday. Just thank God throughout the day for everything, big or small.

Tell God Thank You. I am still here, and God is always with you.

Just be Thankful today, God has been good to us in spite of ourselves.

Do not sit around thinking about what you don't have but think about how Blessed you are for what you do have.

Let's just say "Thank you God for life, good health, and strength."

So many people would like what you have. "Don't take it for granted".

Just be THANKFUL and know that GOD can turn the negative around.

Let's just think about something Good that has happened in your life and SMILE.

ALWAYS find something to be grateful for, especially when it looks like your world is upside down.

Say to yourself "Today is a Wonderful day to be Alive and God is Awesome!"

Look for something Good to come out of every situation of Life.

Thanksgiving is a day to be thankful for family and friends. Enjoy them and love yourself.

Be thankful for people that care about others and are willing to show Love by feeding those who are less fortunate throughout our cities and the world.

Having a wonderful Thanksgiving is a state of mind. Think on something in your life to be Thankful for on this Thanksgiving. God loves you and you are always worthy of His love.

Let's just Thank God for being Good to us even when things don't look good.

I am in a Thankful mood today, working on it being a reality every day.

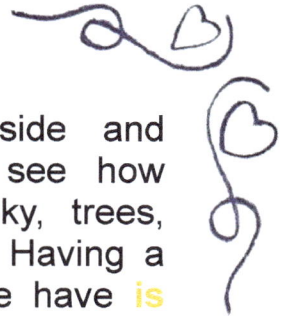

Have you ever gone outside and just stopped to look and see how Beautiful God made the sky, trees, water, and land just for us? Having a heart to Appreciate what we have is Awesome.

This is the day the Lord let us wake up. So, let's be thankful, honor God, and do kind and loving things today.

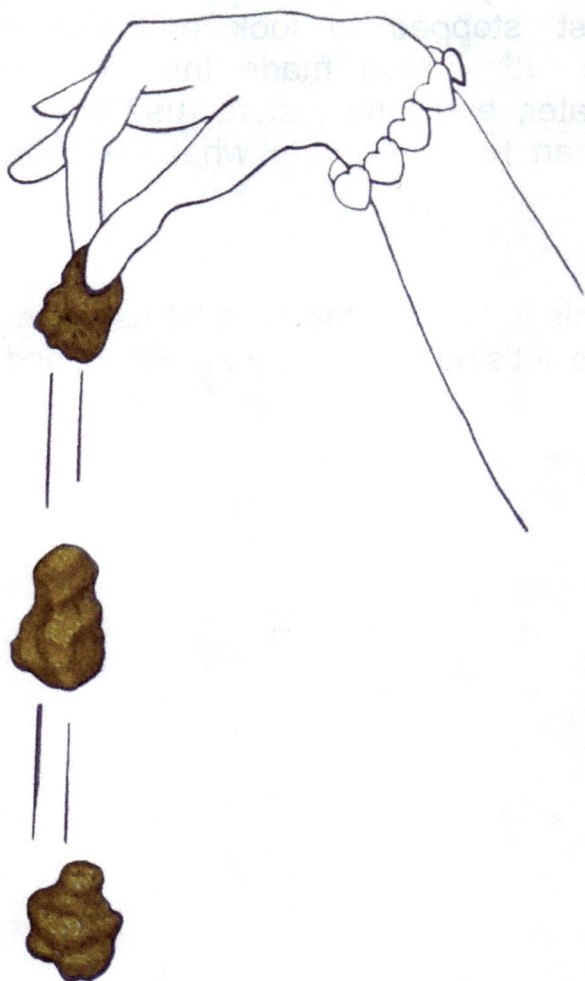

Golden Nuggets 6:

"Did You Ask God?"

Ask God for Guidance in everything you do today.

Let's ask God to rule your day today for everything.

Always ask God to keep you safe. Have an Awesome day!

Don't make any sudden moves when life happens.... Pray First.

Ask God for wisdom before you make your decisions.

If someone is lacking something, don't talk about them. Teach them how to ask God for what they need and Pray.

Did you ever think about why God selected you to be on this earth? Think about Your Purpose and Do it.

When negative situations happen in life take a deep breath, think, ask God for help, get his answer; and then only then make your decision.

We must think like Jesus who did nothing but love in spite of the horrible treatment he received. Can we be like Jesus?

Have you ever had a time that you didn't know what to do? When you do make a decision, be willing to see it through.

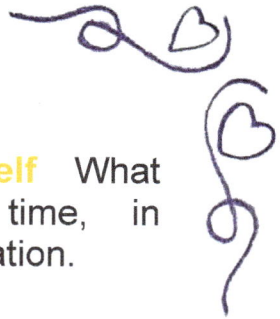

Remember to **ask yourself** What Would Jesus Do every time, in everything, and for every situation.

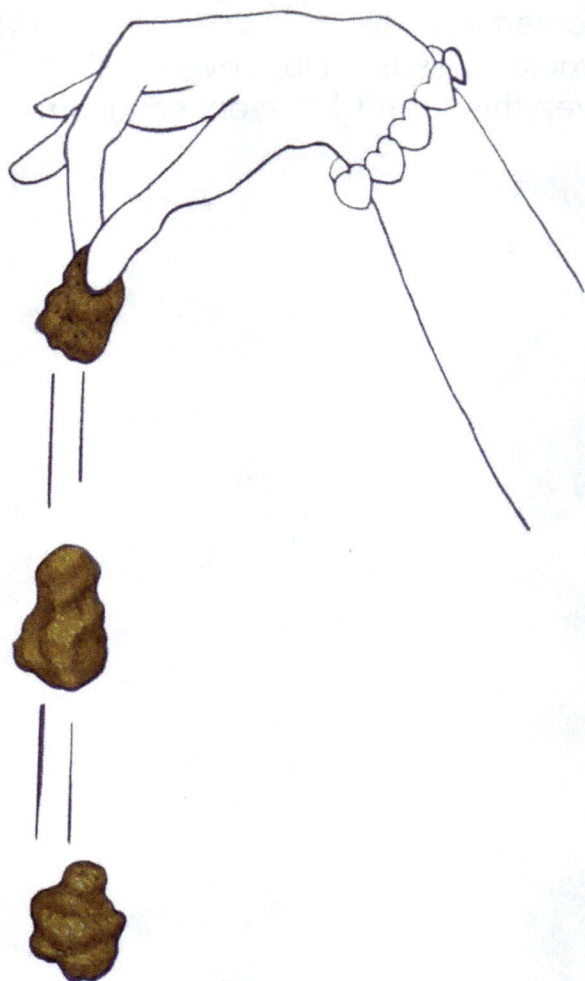

Golden Nuggets 7:

"God's Got It!"

Regardless of your needs, God has them covered all the time.

Say daily, "I walk in God's Protection always."

Remember God protects you when you put him first and are doing the right thing.

Perfect love casts out all fear!!!

Get control of your mind by reading God's word and saying God's word. Believe that God can always handle any situation in His time frame not ours.

You always need Patience. Remember God doesn't always work on our time.

Don't let anyone steal the Dreams that God gives you. Know that God and you are in control of your Destiny.

Don't feel insecure in a new place in life just let God lead you.

Don't look Back on what you had; God is moving you in a New Direction.

It's hard to hear God's voice when you've already decided what you want Him to say.

You have the capability to master all that life throws at you with God's help.

Remember God is able to keep you in All areas of your Life.

Things may not turn out how you want them but, in those times, have Faith because it is going to get Better.

You don't always have to go looking for what you need or want, sometimes it finds you, Believe.

Christ's birth was for us, so we could have a good life even in tough times.

Life can be stressful, but don't let the stress consume you. Just think on good things and let God handle it.

Think on the Birth of Christ because He has done so much for us.

Let God take your problems because He knows what to do with them. Just remember to pray, listen for instructions, and do what He says.

Keep Jesus with you at all times like you do your cell phone.

It's time to receive **presents**, but the biggest present you can receive is **Jesus**.

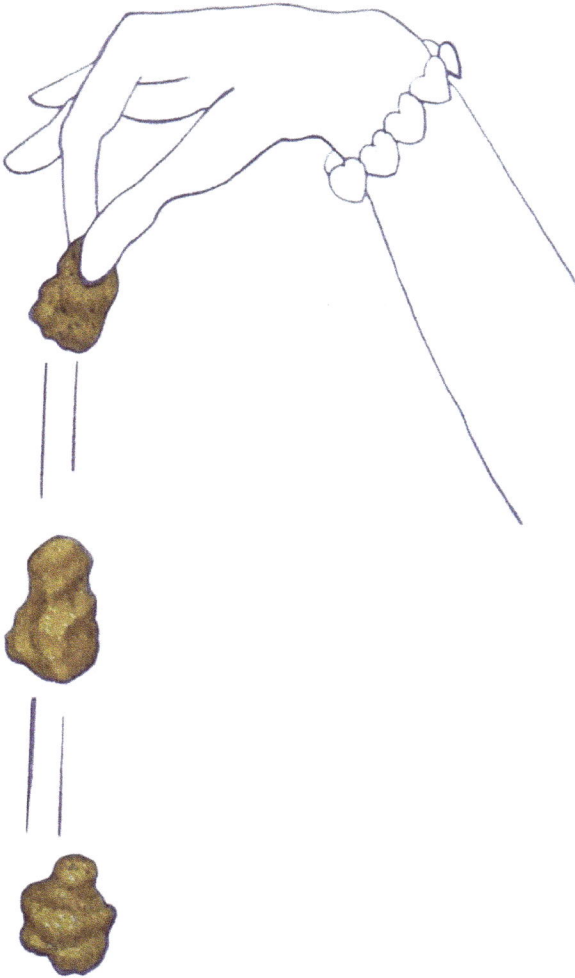

Golden Nuggets 8:

"Walking In Boldness In Prayer"

Don't let fear, doubt, and failure rule you. God has given us power, love, and a sound mind.

Develop your own walk with God. Pray and talk to Him.

Praying is a two-way street; it's talking and Listening to God.

Say a prayer to yourself every day after you wake up. It helps prepare you for the day!!!

Start your day with Prayer and Positive Loving Thoughts.

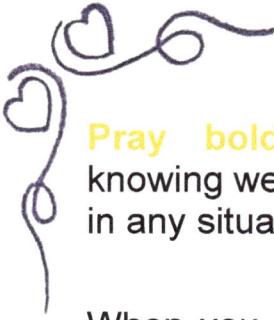

Pray boldly and with confidence knowing we can trust in **God** to intervene in any situation on our behalf.

When you find yourself judgmental and unforgiving towards others, ask yourself what would you do if **God** felt like that towards you.

God created the universe and still cares about each of us. Pray as if you believe.

Worship and Prayer strengthen our faith. Thank **God** for who He is and for blessing us with every spiritual blessing through Christ.

It is so important to have Godly Prayer Warriors to help sustain you when there is a severe loss or crisis in your life.

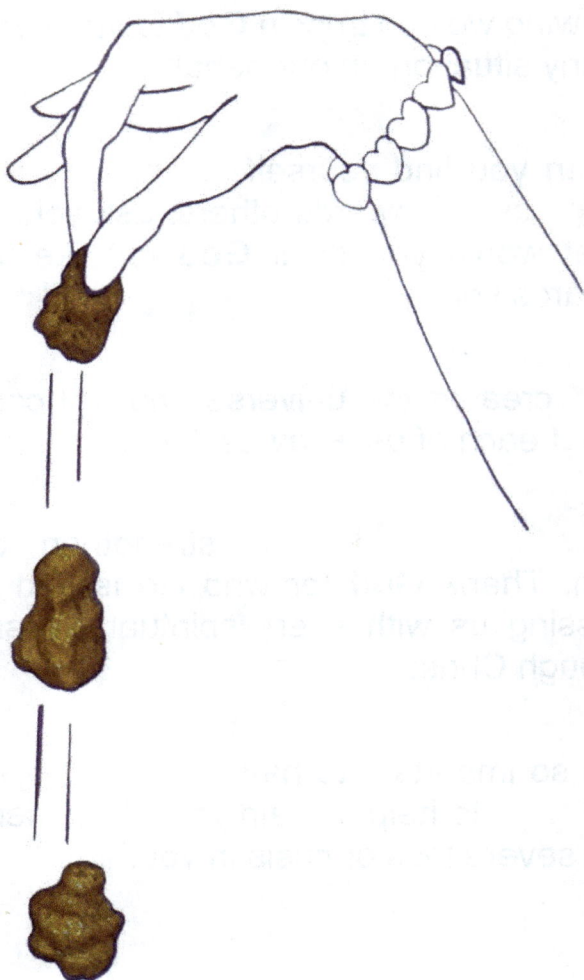

Golden Nuggets 9:

"Extra Sugar On Top Wisdom"

Friday is the start of the weekend. Relax, have fun, and always be RESPECTFUL AND COMPASSIONATE.

Remember you are a Blessing to us, and please remember that you are Loved.

The path you are on in life is designed for you and you alone.

Sometimes you feel as if no one cares or you are not valued. Trust me, we have all been there.

We didn't grow up under the same parental rules so give each other some slack.

Right is right and wrong is wrong. Do right, no matter what it is.

Remember that God loves you, so let's honor Him by showing Love.

Today is a wonderful day to be alive even if everything is not going your way.

One of the Biggest Lessons in Life: Don't ever think it can't happen to you!!!

Don't let the bad days overshadow your good days. You will make it through these also.

Remember that things are going to come out alright. When there is trouble, just keep walking forward one step at a time.

To help stop frustration, try thinking ahead and doing tasks early.

Manage your time with a sense of urgency. You will be surprised how much you can accomplish.

It's so easy to waste money given to you, but when you work for it, you will see the difference.

To make great decisions, use your money, time, and energy wisely with forethought.

Positive thoughts should be put into action.

Love God first and then yourself. Make sure you love everyone as God does.

Know that every problem starts out as a THOUGHT and is TEMPORARY. Work through it. Things always change and change will come.

Forget the bad and focus on the good.

It is important that you spend time with God daily.

You will have failures in life, but you don't have to be a failure. Get up and try again.

Going back isn't always the same as you remember it.

Don't let how you've been conditioned in the past stop your future; you don't always know what the future holds.

Make sure you read a Bible verse daily to get God's help and guidance.

If you read your BIBLE, you will be surprised by the information you can learn on how to live.

Whatever you do behind someone's back you are also doing in front of God's eyes.

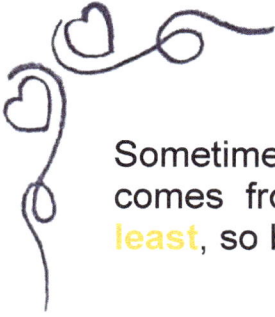

Sometimes what we need the most comes from where we expect it the least, so be watchful.

Everything comes to you in the right moment, just be Patient.

Even the most intense storm in your life has a breaking point (Stand Fast). You never know where life will lead you!!!

A Joyful Heart will chase away sorrow or sadness.

Sometimes doors are closed for reasons that we will never know but where there's faith there's hope. Hang onto hope because another door will open - Hope!!!

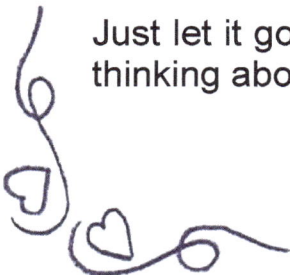

Just let it go - Don't ruin a Good Day by thinking about a bad yesterday.

When a negative situation arises and you don't know what to do, give it time because Time can heal everything.

You are in charge of Your Happiness. Don't let anyone trick you out of it.

Not everyone's advice is good. Ask God for guidance to have an Amazing life that empowers You.

Smile - Life is short, enjoy it while you have it.

Love should be shown in EVERY situation of our lives UNCONDITIONALLY.

School can be challenging sometimes but it is a means to an end. Apply yourself!!!

Stay Calm, it's okay not to have everything figured out, things will work out in the proper time.

Our most difficult times often lead to our greatest moments.

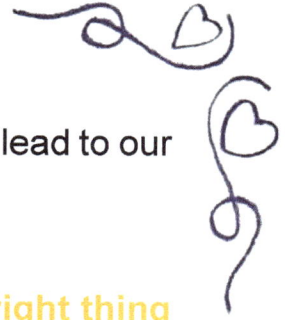

Sometimes, we can't see the right thing because we only see what we want.

www.ingramcontent.com/pod-product-compliance
Lightning Source LLC
Chambersburg PA
CBHW072212090426

42740CB00012B/2489